Alphabet Theater

Wesleyan Poetry

Alphabet Theater

PERFORMANCE POETRY

Meredith Stricker

Wesleyan University Press
Middletown, Connecticut

Published by Wesleyan University Press, Middletown, CT 06459
© 2002 by Meredith Stricker
Printed in the United States of America
5 4 3 2 1
Library of Congress Control Number: 2002115042

acknowledgments

"The Lightning Hive" and "The Still Place" texts have appeared in their entirety in issues of *Epoch*. "Island" and "bee mother" from "The Lightning Hive" series have also appeared in the Milkweed Editions Anthology *Looking For Home*, while "bee mother" is reprinted in the Norton anthology *Mother Songs*. Video stills from this series: "the bee hum of all languages" and "the bee's language" appeared in *The Iowa Review*. "The Still Place" with another version of images has also appeared in *rooms*. *"The Poor Body"* text was published in *Pavement* and was performed in collaboration with Elizabeth Lahey at PostMasters Gallery, New York.

*For Elizabeth Lahey, in collaboration over the years
and also for the maze and lights held in the field.*

We do not need any more actors directors playwrights designers critics. We do not need any more love, hate, psychology, politics, history, space, intimacy, stages, or especially money.

We need so much that we can't need anything but a theatre of the mind.

Crawl through the dark cave of mind that is the womb of all theatre and you will discover the theater of the mind. The theater of the mind is the loudest, brightest, most theatrical space in all of creation. It is collective and individual, invisible and all envisioning, narcissistic and universal, beautiful and ugly and brutal and tender; it is the only theatrical hope/experience that keeps us going back and back, performance after putrid performance; it is why we love to read the plays of Shakespeare, to enact the magic incantation of their story heart and language smell in our minds and why so often their stagings disappoint, frustrate and limit our imaginings. The theater of the mind is the stage of perfect wonder that each one of us and every one of us ever smitten by live performance longs to see again, a lost Eden that comes so easily in our secret thought and appears so hard to realize on theliving stage. And it is a tragedy — this loss of a live, transformative theater, this cavern of twisting into labyrinth into gorge into ocean and sky because we need its external presence as a people, as community to act in the very fact of its occurring as omen, talisman, catalyst, to dream out the potentiality of life, to dream a new blue print of civilization, together.

— Shelley Berc, *Theater of the Mind*

Contents

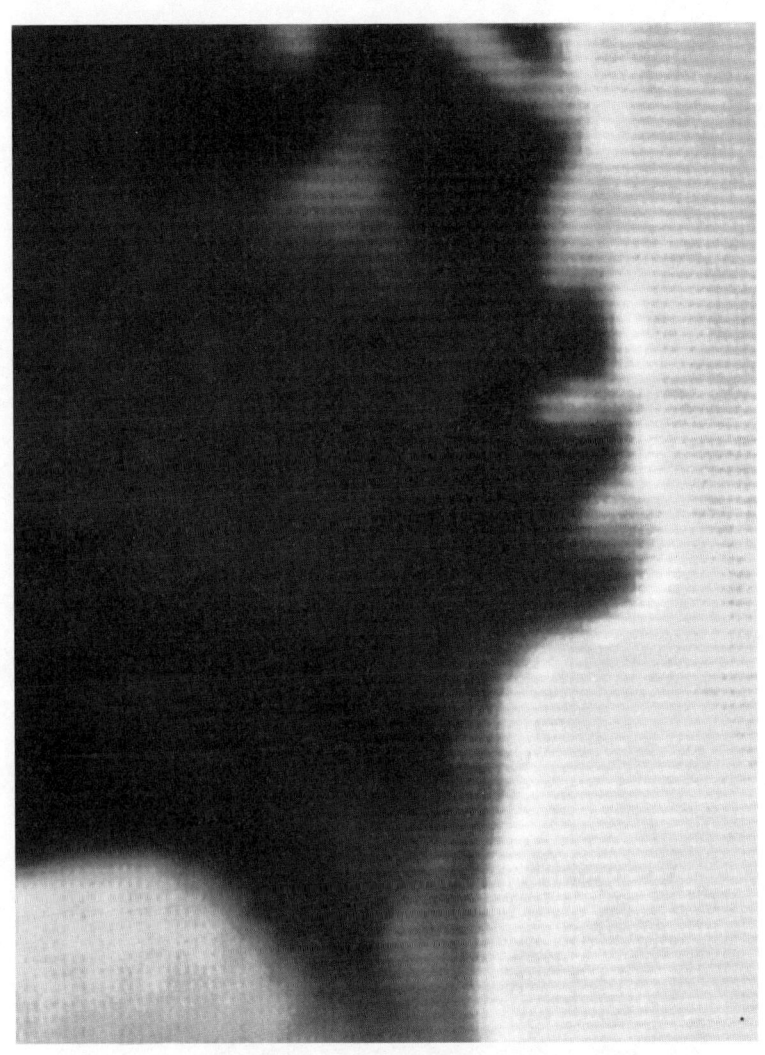

The Poor Body

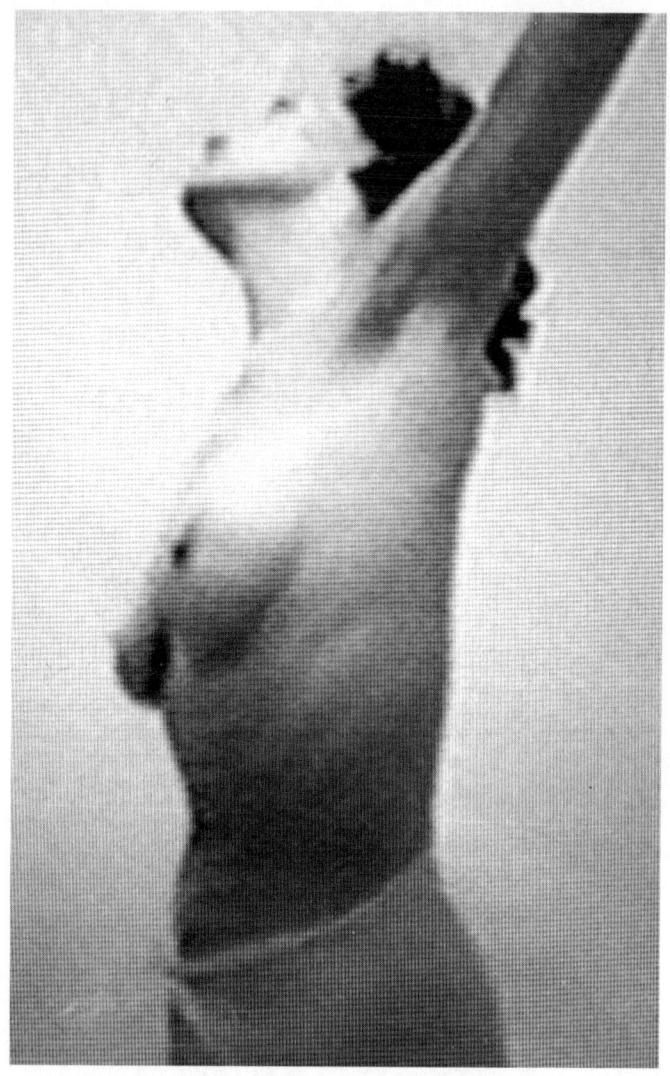

THE POOR BODY

AVE

Ave dirt, one thousand cracked thornbushes, ave

Lady of the House, her arms folded across

thin acrylic sweater, ave

small voice, unintended saplings

ave sisters, one quarter, one quarter, the blunt

palm of my hand turned upwards

as her phases, reeling

turn (faces) to earn

a healing — cup, white

(washed out) (luckless)

as in *orexia*,

'what we long for'

a moon there, her faces, ave

An avenue

as in reaching for

A way is a cup

She steadies herself

and leans toward this

thin blue bone china

teacup, gold-trimmed & clean

A way is a cup

if there's an opening, spirit

rushes toward the newly emptied

place, as an open palm means gift

she psalms a new measure

The power of positive

as money appears

greenly as a pear tree

free as unzoned honey

oh majesty of purple grains

tis of thee, a way: ore

lucite, agnite, ignite, vein or

(a d'or ation) (a door)

away — solemnly the way

discreet money rustles — wings of it, or

A blank way, the path closed

pauper cup: empty no harvested

paper cup: crushed, foolish, reaped

to zero — blocked — blacking Ex

haus ted X'ed out

No dough Na — da

cause Demeter

wintered the grain

increasing poverty

the poor pouring

riches increasing

unheard of

empty gain

no grain

auctioned

rain

initiate

pain

sane

as

an-

not one

n

N. = (CUP)

n.

where n. means

born

 &

nephew

 &

new

nominative

 &

noon

normal

 &

north

northern

 &

noun

 &

number

ave! n.

thou most reduced

of moon

of beggarly

cup — oh and overfilling white

you hold one

(sandy dirt part way up)

where it lives

(sand colored thorns, thinnest nipples)

cactus flesh

(the uneaten desert)

treasure — sea green fin, firetooth

(baked, fired — as ceramic)

but raw still, uneaten

Still & steady

yet you flower — what thinking

spare thou in desert chests of certain

dirt. Thou, ammunition of not moving, aim of sharp

fixity. She sharpens (shark)

water (someone's lost

or spirited water)

Whitens her entirely dry body

she's an

icon to water

absented

water, her

inside name

wa - wa - wa - wa

rapt

waterer

rein — pure reign

narrow (*νερο*)

wet

(wit)

ness

not violate her

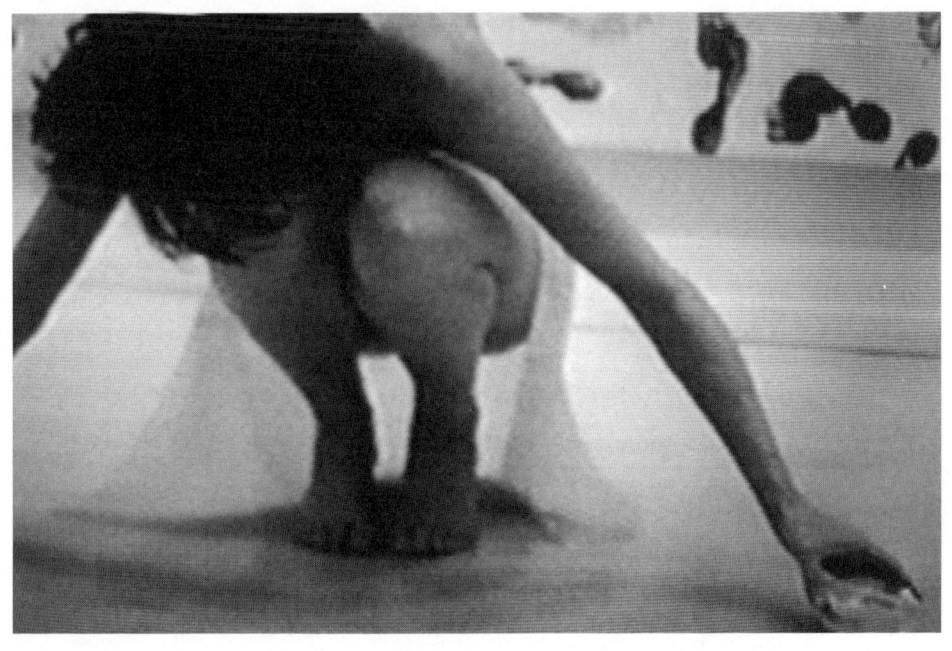

And you don't walk on my table, no desert

lightning heightens you, yet you survive

suburbia's verbia. And don't talk

or seize or read, breathing

More slowly. Mating, 'self-propagating,' priestly

Hollowed. Hallowed. Splinter, tallow

thou ash green candle, a screen for what

soul-crate painted box plant. Root bound, you kneel

not before us. Fierce plant, secretest one, cactus

Fact that we trust. Solid — you opaque this still life

"What are she?" What being sheds her here, not grain

unusual, unusable. A watcher

Splintery icon. Dark, lunarative

Silent as ink. Not troubled, troubling

Unharvested — poor body, she's also a figure

the rich one, the poor one in her anti

abundance, she never dances. Fruitless

a-parently (not american plains)

She's all fruited: *agave, signero,*

candle, mescal, nopales, prickly pear — plain

she explains   painted soul crate   tell me your nature

in your words   your nature   in your own

THE POOR BODY
PostMasters Gallery, New York, 1986
choreographed & performed by Elizabeth Lahey
text, sound, & stills: Meredith Stricker
videography: Frederic Lahey

Soundtrack of cicadas rising and falling, constant. Sheepbells at dusk on Lesbos, running in the distance and closer, deeper. Percussive cascade of bells against the roar of wind over dirt paths and thistles.

The text is read slowly, rhythmically into this landscape of heat & oleandered springs, becoming a map for movement.

A woman walks toward us — the poor body: a cactus or moon, our mother, an anorexic girl, Queen of Heaven, carcass, living pearl.

She follows the sound of bells and heat, spiraling like a DNA helix, spinning with increasing intensity, opening and closing, filling and emptying: *<as her phases, reeling>*

<turn (faces) to earn>   *<a healing - cup, white>*   *<(washed out) (luck-less)>*   *<a moon there, her faces, ave>*

She lifts her arms & reaches out — an *orexia*

whittled down to **n**, beyond nothing

cup overflowing = desert

she, holy cactus blooming

The Lightning Hive

the bee hum of all languages

THE LIGHTNING HIVE

dedicated to Bolek Grezsyncski, of The Living Museum:
artist, actor, human being, whose loss is immeasurable

To take form as a semiotic opera. Not minimalist, but as baroque as possible to create a sense of a three-dimensional hive: threaded through with voice, call and response, electronic and acoustic music.

The principal characters are letters of the alphabet: "A" and its variations, the liquid "L": current English forms along with archaic prototypes. Saussure's signifier and signified are choreographed as lightning and thunder, who are also active characters throughout.

Some of the letters take the form of bees, who become part of an insect chorus — the shirring hum and sounds of approaching weather akin to Artaud's rendering of Balinese theater: *"this excessive heiraticism with its sliding alphabet, its screams like splitting rock, its sounds of wood being chopped and logs being rolled, creates, in the air, in space, visually as well as aurally a kind of physical and animated drone. And after a moment the magical identification is made: we know it is we who are speaking."*

Ultraviolet light ("the color bees see") is used between some of the scenes to give a sense of twilight or dawn, the fading transcription of afterimages. The voices of the chorus shift in and out of focus imitating in range the multiple vision of the bee's composite eye to the almost blind intensity of a single speaker.

trompe l'oeil

fresco

cobalt & ochre & cochineal & titanium

paint made of dirt & insects

immaculate

glistening image

you carry in the palm of your hand

breathing space

her head lit up

river speeding sideways

wet brushstrokes faster than

the thing, the thing itself

god have mercy

that things touch

is our most human science

& beautiful & false

we hear

color

the earliest noise

to spill world into our eyes

unmediated

correspondence

how shiny the painted

merciful

leaves

are

□ 午

and now is our chanting useless?

       I ask   for the blessing

          what we hold in common

             blessure or wound

the **A** of Ave   are we losing her?

     start again with the cave
           entrance
                                 letters, handprints
the sun grows colder & brighter

                                 red clay dust
                                 & black ash

                               outlast the god

   I count on you more & more

       what's real
               cracks
       stand by it

    the bird calling   co - here
              co - here

     the ghosts of Pound and Eliot

       both lost

  but not the A, earliest letters

          as a shadow chorus

     behind everything we write or say or read

             cemetery
                    our alphabet
new white bed   thick light

     to be allowed so close

      to remember
              the one who comes up on her own
   motion, green Kore
        "Orpheus irrelevant to her rising"

cypress trees bend in the fierce storm

        our joy knowing weeds in this landscape —

      but not their names
                    owl in grove

                newt on muddy trail
light that pours

through the center of this house

        significant accidents are all I can save

three sisters climb out of saltwater, wet and unashamed

      to face their mother

there's the three of them make, each standing figure

        each line

not one-to-one correspondence

    but correspondence all the same

      there are many ways in

        your

        <u>birth</u>
cut open geode   day   the letters A
                                        V
                                        E

     more new red

        climbing roses

        & I will praise

      these thorns, these exact

"this tiny insect life portal to another"
Dickinson

drë
drë
drë

      you are the shape forming my ears
         you hollow hearing
           yellow, crisp

--- ---
--- ---   [whispered]   crowding the interstices, clinging
--- ---   to leaves to make us hear
--- ---   closeness & closeness
--- ---   ever springing up
--- ---   from silence
--- ---
--- ---

dry water (crickets)
drë drë drë
hiss hose bush full of wet birds
[cicadas]
       sink
muddy
[hesitation]   drëë
[stutter]   drëë
as in stepping   - - - -   [insistent]
and stubbing   - - - -
your shoe   - - - -
against the threshold   - -
surprised

                       all that my ear knows
                          is the sound
                          of insects
  winged islands   thousands of little saints
                    instruct us to become fliers
                      like themselves
                so tight and smooth, black
                    and very light

drr

      drr   drr   mismanagement
      drr   drr   surely not in this
[louder]   drr   drr   spectacular buzzing
      drr   drr   no government
                             only rhythm

      [going forward]

ice   all of them speak
ice
ice

      wind moves through

voice devotion for hours   [and we call them insects,
          instead of worshippers]

                        in - sects

          intersect

ta tw tw - whrrr   twisting ⌇⌇⌇⌇
      [underneath]

wrrr   like an electric element
        heating up — metallic
        pure pitch

      [increasing]
            to a sharp knot

sweep sweep   the new ones rise up
sweep sweep

          apples ripen, alive with the sound
          of white cabbage moths

dddd drzzz   dddd   drzzz
   t tt   t   t   t   t

                   t

   h   bieu bieu bieu
   e
   a
see[r]ing

                    our language
                          imitates - intimates
                              our mother

                                          whom we gaze into
                                              listen into

                        our mother daddy-long-legs

            chuk
                    chuk   [faster]
      chuk
              chuk

                              a swinging up and over — all sound — visible

  drzz   drzz   listen to the leaves make all this

          drzz   noise — without them no sound, no voice

                                          only branches

                              shaking like skeletons in the wind

☐ ISLAND

for Eva Rath Stricker

Taken away from her language
she is islanded in white
space, beautiful dove island
the poor body stranded here
wants to speak her first
sounds: *égy ketö haram*
the numbers, *négy öt hat* —
all broken away from her
so that she may live.
They tell her she is lucky
when so many others have perished
now her tongue translates
automatically. She is lucky
to live like Eurydice
not dead exactly — just displaced.
We try so hard to stay alive, above ground
but it's not clear if the earth
will survive us, we love her so much
our gaze dissolves her — some of her water
some of her air — we could even blow her up
all at once, the way Orpheus
loved Eurydice. I hated him
for looking back, but he is no safer
than any one of us, our Orpheus
torn & acrid vines burn, bleeding from empty
sockets, his head, his lyre wash up on Lesbos
"thy floating singer late" and where
did Hart Crane wash ashore —
his head, his lyre floating forever in the word.
The more a thing is torn
the more places it can connect.

The poor body — fragile as Sappho's lost
text, taken from her language into
another life? We want to believe
it will never end
it will never end.
Already we are swimming toward
an island we say we can never drown
if life stays alive, we will read
her back to us, whole again, if life
survives us, the body will
be our book and keep on
singing.

(from a Hungarian dictionary)

MOTHER	–	anya, méh
MÉH	–	bee; womb, uterus
méhébe fogadni	–	to conceive
méhállás	–	hive, shed
méhanya	–	uterus
méhbaj	–	hysteria, fits of the mother
méhbefogadás	–	conception
méhbeli	–	uterine
méhcsípés	–	sting of a bee
méhdüh	–	uterine fury
méhgörcs	–	spasms in hysteria
méhgörcsös	–	hysterical
méhgyümölcs	–	fruit of the womb
méhház	–	bee house, apiary
méhhüvely	–	vagina
méhkirálynő	–	queen bee
méhkosár	–	bee hive
méhmagzat	–	embryo, fetus
méhraj	–	swarm of bees
méhrajzás	–	swarming of bees
méhser	–	honey wine
méhszáj	–	mouth of the womb
méhtenyésztés	–	bee farming
méhtükör	–	speculum
méhüszög	–	false conception

in my mother's lost language

it suddenly becomes clear

the hive we are born into

the bee hum

of all languages

we speak or will never hear

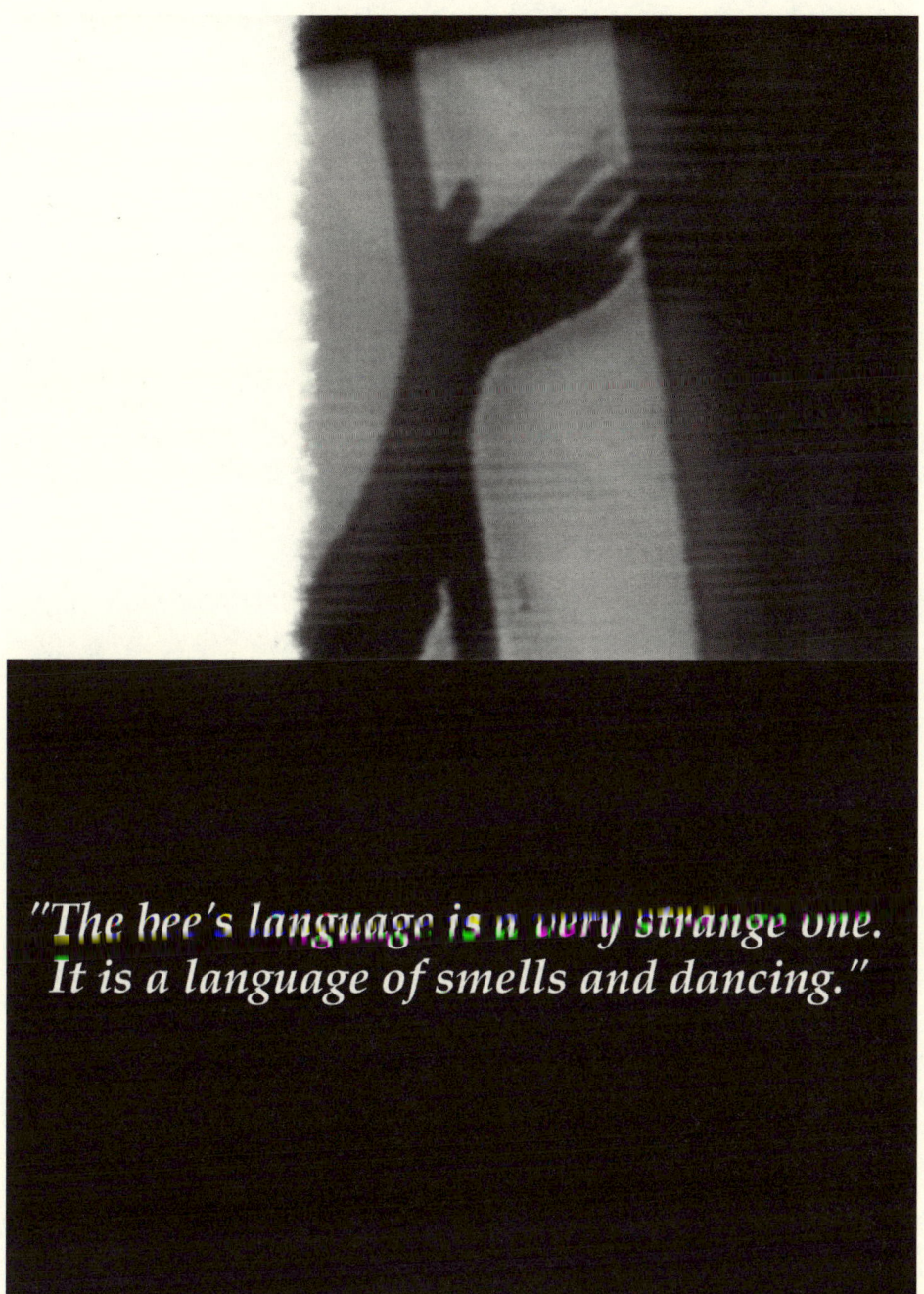

"The bee's language is a very strange one.
It is a language of smells and dancing."

"The bee's language is a very strange one.
It is a language of smells and dancing."

□

to crack the code bees swarm

we lean further into green air

to read the honeycombed alphabet

we turn our eyes back

toward the skull

a delirium of reading

into this waxy site

saint's flesh

a theater of bees

thea - trikon

seeing - place

where all we see are these letters

"bees see a color we cannot even imagine"

smeared with her scent

through the many cells

a color we see into imagining

bees are letters in flight

each sound a figure

"a light and winged and holy thing"

round and round in a maze

of narrow circles

which is the book we dive into

we don't know where the bee maps will carry us

as we dance our hive

we lose our way on the way to pollen

☐   Inexhaustible furnaces of grass

green cities

mill insects & light, gouge intricate dirt.

The rasp of their industry

rattles aluminum laundry lines

where painter's pants stiffen spreadeagled

& short sleeved shirts flutter. Underwear relaxes.

Such stubborn & pure laundry

hums toward the floating shade

like two-dimensional boats, a little breathless.

My neighbor's clothes are figures in my own dreams

I can understand them in the same way

aslant

intimate — untouchable shapes.

Aristotle could

make fine categories for them

for what the body casts away

from itself

these shadows of disgust, longing & pride

semaphore to us

we want to return, they say

to our original   human home

☐ At night
   opposites attract
   flow through the hidden, liquid "l"
   where laundry is replaced by lightning,
   aluminum poles suddenly
   crack, naked
   as though x-rayed
   a switching on & off
   stimulus
   response
   or a longing, a leap, an "l"
   the veins radiant in Thoreau's leaf
   or lief — gladly, willingly —
   desire of the world for form, arc to arc — bright white
   we suffer from this bridge of lightning to loss

☐ The word is made of other words:
   laundry carries *lavage, lawn, laundress and launch.*
   The word's a small vessel set in water to be jostled by
   the *lavandere* — washer of linen. And the verbs — *lave,*
   wash, bathe — tunnel inside a heap — a hive — of clothes
   like details of stitching & bones
   burned into black *lava.*
   A current of "l" quickens
   to a field of *lavender* in red clay soil.
   Here is the color bees see — ultraviolet
   humming invisible to us in the words
   we speak everyday.

☐ Later sound arrives.
  We have grown fearful waiting
  in the breach between lightning & thunder — conscience
  splits, self watches self.
  The written is loosened
  or loose or lost from the spoken.
  There's only a track of shiny field corn
  spilled over asphalt to guide us.
  But sound is everything.
  We're like the angry blind man at the bus stop
  in early morning snow. "Tie my shoe. I'm blind"
  he shouts, thrashing his way into traffic.
  "That's not the bus stop," someone tells him.
  He gets angrier and louder: "tie my shoe."

  The bee is a sign never so far
  from its own sound.
  Imagine a way
  to draw thunder to us.
  Tie a string to a bit of wood
  & whirl it over your head at initiation rites.
  Monstrous insect drone
  roars from the unseen.
  You are blind
  & hold the whirring
  leash tied to god.
  Listener,
  you are washed
  away by
  voice.

☐ It's as though there's a gap we could die in
  and the days go on. Cherry trees are blooming & lilacs
  lean against the porch. We walk over dry corn fields
  half stumbling on clods of dirt & root clumps.
  Maybe there'll be pheasants under the pines.
  Maybe we'll discover this is real after all.
  A tiny crack opens.
  The eggs are dyed scarlet red.
  Infinitesimal seam we notice
  unconsciously, if at all.
  At this feast, the lamb's eyes stare & stare.

  Smell of iris in a closed room.
  Falling petals stick like skin onto each other.
  Intimation of another shore, quietly rotting.
  Lightning bugs, misty air, sudden rainfall.

  To wake at dawn with immense clarity.

  Like passing trucks full of hogs on the interstate,
  seeing their noses rummage through metal slats
  so alive in their bodies next to us.
  A blue Mercury sedan on the other side
  blurs traffic as though we could die
  eyes wide open, unbelieving.
  "Here I am,"
  a man declares
  before bolt strikes him dead.
  There was no thunder, lightning or sign
  of lightning before the killer bolt struck.

  Did he reach heaven like a fairground
  where Mennonites gather in gauze bonnets
  looking like cafeteria workers, where swarms
  of Anabaptists auction quilts, lamb sausage
  & shoo-fly pie under acres of yellow lights?
  Or is this where we've crossed over
  into our own lives where no lightning strikes
  us open as if we could ever die.

☐   Before the god there was the monster *Brontos*

               thunderer — HE

          "the sacred is the father of god" — and the mother

                  willow grove survives

          surprises   the god

as letters,

         hieroglyphs   survive

               the words or sense

     return to the hive

               close your mouth to speak

    archaic chorus

        magnet

      for the Muse — harmonium

of bees inscribing perfect hemispheres.

        They outline two lobes in the air

  to describe far-away lilies.

        The shape of a human brain in the air

     contours the language of distance for bees

       as though we wandered like ghosts in their comb

all those rooms — rim of shells — each cell

a mirror

to find our way out of there.

"We are the bees of the Invisible"

can't see out

such fear I have never known before

just to reach the sidewalk

faint-hearted, no steps

carry me to the other side

flurry of wings — water not body

"the feare of things invisible is

the naturall seed of religion"

a fear that draws the feared

into itself — thunderer

that power — virtú —

"as of a shy bird hard to catch"

all animate & inanimate life

the seen & the unseen

"a fragment of anything to its entirety"

carries the whole,

emptying

□ to contact this opening
oceans spill into
why he says why write
so fast why
so busy
we see things different
the host waits in the chair across from you
he is inside you
inside you
this one
not you
everything
you are
everything
roses calling roses to mind
in dead winter
the immense bee hum
of white washed dome
dusty kelp rubbed on your hands
hot springs, all
inside
this
telling
this
inward
well-
spring
bells
make us hear
silence
is the active rain
pouring through
frozen snowfields
this moment
I'm alive

silence is the active rain

Staging Notes

HIDDEN ALPHABET

Letters from hundreds of language systems are projected onto the labyrinthine forms of the stage to produce the effects of a very large living hive. Aramaic, Sumerian, Quichu, early Chinese, overlay Finnish, Urdu, Ainu characters in slides and film projections ranging from black and white to overlays of pigments and markings: painted and incised glyphs.

The effect is one of rushing downstream, flotsam and artifacts stream past us: the image for the *palm of the hand*, for *shelter*, for *stars.* It's suddenly as though we could no longer contain our language inside of us, as though words became mountains: immeasurable and exterior to us. As though we inhabit and move inside of language rather than encompass words moving through us.

There's a white bed in a cave. Three sisters move and speak from a landscape of cave paintings and handprints. sticks are choreographed to form letters:

INSECTS

The stage is emptied, leaving space for wind and the Chorus: an overlay of insect and human voices — crickets, cicadas, bees and 40 or more performers. The sounds are relayed from many amplifiers throughout the theater: overhead and underfoot, rising to an incantatory, vibrating drone.

Closing to afterimages in violet light. The Chorus holds up branches of dry leaves, rattling them in the sound of the wind.

ISLAND

Dark, except for candles, the stage is quiet, spare. A woman sits in an old European chair: my Hungarian mother/Eurydice-Eva. She is dressed in white, abstracted, speaking of herself as though of someone else. In the background, the sound of Hungarian phonemes overlap on many tracks, like the murmur of running water. As she speaks, the woman turns on an old projector. The film stutters toward us on a transparent scrim: grainy scenes from pre-War Hungary and wartime newsreels and stills, scenes from mythology: Orpheus, Eurydice — equally distant and close to us as these black and white documentary photographs.

The screen turns to images of fast moving river currents, as the figure onstage appears as though behind and underwater.

BEE MOTHER

The insect chorus returns to the cave site: speaking and singing in several cycles of English and Hungarian phrases, at first separately and distinctly, then with increasing overlay, becoming fused with the sound of bees flooding in from various locations throughout the theater. The last phrases are spoken or sung by a single speaker in English and the voice merges with the increasing intensity of the bee hum.

"A LANGUAGE OF SMELLS & DANCING"

The insect Chorus sings and moves through an intricate choreography, on the ground and in the air, vertical and upside down. The stage is filled with light and pollen and takes on the appearance of an illuminated manuscript, with the bees as moving letters.

38

INEXHAUSTIBLE FURNACES OF GRASS

The stage becomes a very bright, green field, with laundry lines stretched across in all directions like a spider web. These lines can move freely, with garments floating on them: gauzy, empty, eloquent figures. Some of the clothes are inhabited and begin to speak.

AT NIGHT   THE WORD IS MADE OF OTHER WORDS

Lightning activates the stage and leads into a short film, projected very large: words crack open into other words tracing their own interior etymologies as though x-rayed. Images of a boat turn into fields of lavender, of laundry becoming lava, of bees*******************The entire theater is flooded with violet and then black light, along with the rising of the at first imperceptible sound of bees. This increasing hum is experienced as a vibration rather than sound, the seats and stage vibrate and hum. Everything is changing color and form.

LATER SOUND ARRIVES

The theater goes blind with darkness. Onstage, a single performer becomes visible incrementally, slowly as the movement of a flower opening, speaking while coming into focus, spinning the bullroarer overhead. The movement and sound of the bullroarer are pinpointed, and also enlarged by mirrors and monitors tracking the motion in close-up, in stills.

IT'S AS THOUGH THERE'S A GAP

The sound of the bullroarer fades as images of letterforms are interspersed with enormous, almost holographic close-ups of: a red egg, the fading bloom of an iris, fast-moving traffic, the startled faces of livestock in slatted trucks. The staging and singers are very "operatic": elaborately costumed and lit. A man is struck by lightning while singing impressively and futilely. Lightning flares out from his body like a torch and fills the theater. The stage turns into paradise. We've crossed over, are suspended in a place where everything is slow, calm, unreal: a place of orderly lawns and many varieties of pie.

BEFORE THE GOD

Paradise becomes the interior of a vast honeycomb: lit up the color of amber and wax, echoing with thunder. The Bee Chorus returns: at least one hundred performers — some carrying mirrors to reflect each other and the honeycombed theater and audience. Others carry bullroarers which they whirl overhead to a crescendo of whirring hum. The choreograhpy is intricate, imitating the figure-eight infinity loop   of bees communicating the locations of flowers and pollen to others in the hive. A sign language of bees, accompanied by the sung text and rising hum of bullroarers and chorus. Movement and sound increase their intensity to a sudden blackout, followed by the violet glow of black light. The stage retains and plays back afterimages as the retina would: flashing stills unreel on video monitors throughout.

TO CONTACT THIS OPENING

In the ultraviolet dark, the stagelight focuses on a single speaker. Other members of the Chorus become visible gradually, illuminated by the mirrors they carry or by the strings of their bullroarers which light up as they whirl them overhead. Movements are minimal, quiet. Sounds of rustling, humming — almost imperceptible. The singing is clear, unhurried — in between speech and song, in the manner of Mahler lieder. It's as though someone were speaking very close to our ear. As though we were thinking rather than hearing the words. As the text progresses, the singer begins to take on wings, becoming a kind of large, human bee: Eros, perhaps, or one of the unsaved angels. Bells sound as lightning flashes across violet-white snowfields. Lit up snow falls over the darkened stage and audience: scraps of the performance text: letterforms, images. The last lines — "*This moment I'm alive*" — echoes as — "*I'm a hive*" — in our hearing.

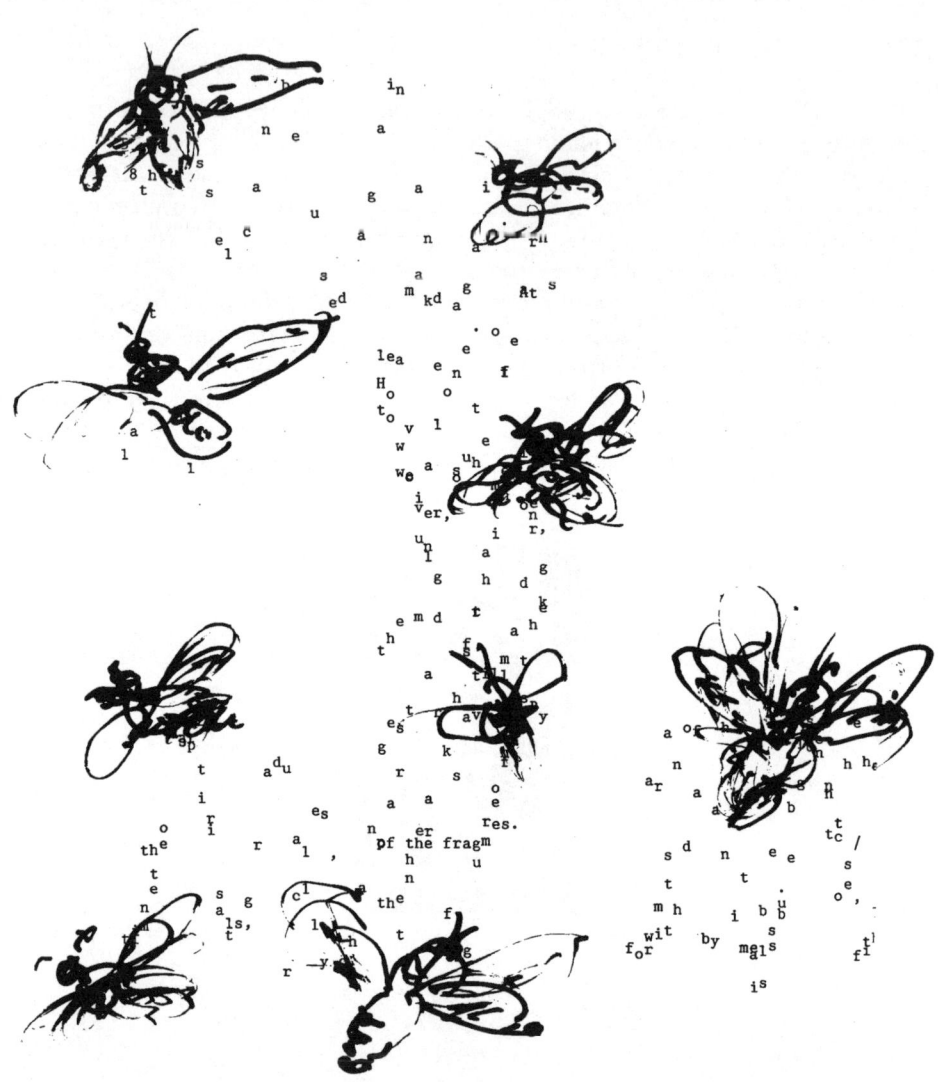

42

The Still Place

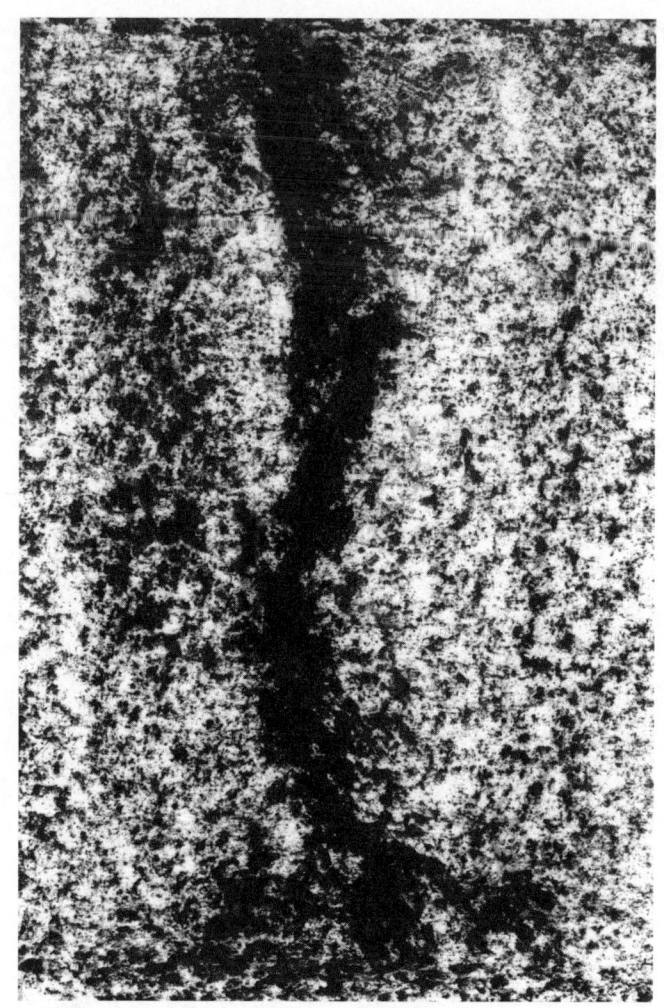

THE STILL PLACE

Takes place in the interstices of the everyday: a car ride, lightning storm, front door of the family home where the son is turned away, photo albums and electron microscope pictures of the living and the dead.

Everything hinges on the absolute and fragile border of skin, the porous boundary between "is" & "is not," between "I" & "you." When we enter the interior of the word *skin*, we find *scissors* & *scar*, configuring a holding together that is identical to its own loosening and unbinding: *scissors* to *knot*, *healing* to *wound*. The sense of being hurled by the edge of our skin into and out of extinction.

Occasionally, the lines are voiced or spoken aloud. Primarily the text is sounded as a series of interior voices performed as we read.

Death, with a briefcase

The Car, our best friend

The Storm, inclusive of all

Red Salamander, the witness

◻, B — the letter for House

Stillness, at any moment:
the exact place occupied; see also *fate*

Skin, Scissors: sharing the same
root words, entangled

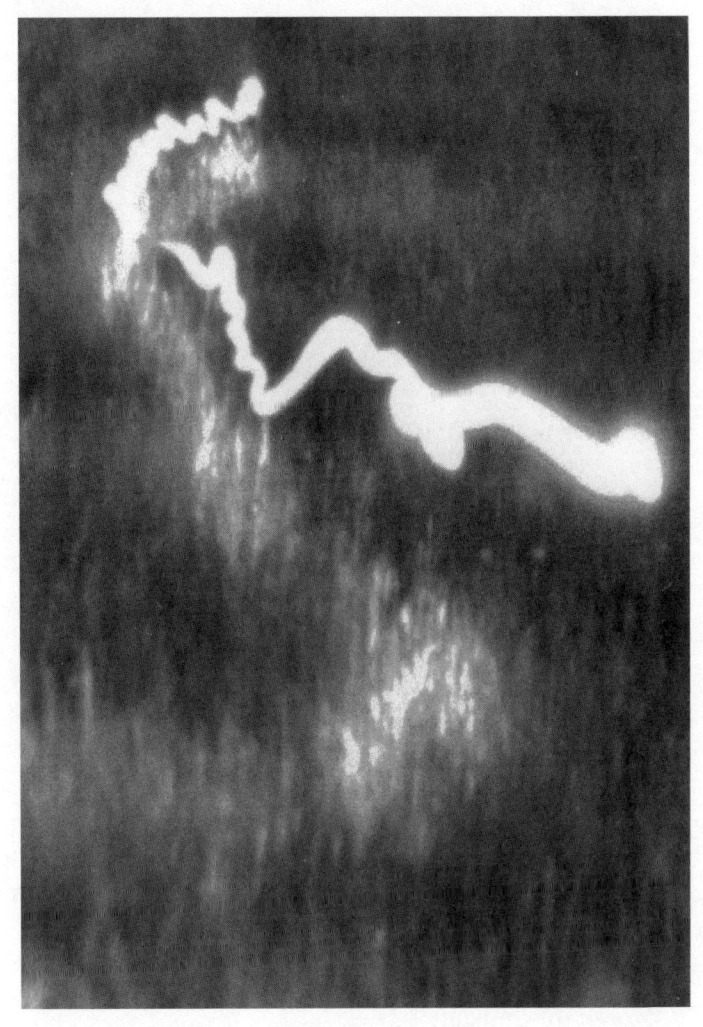

47

Red salamander, death is

Spill apart, echo, improve upon

Death is the most active character —
getting things done

Successful. Male or female

They are moving toward a friend who waits for them

(The storm) is the still place

Osmosis, chain reaction . . . reverses

Some of the speaking moves inside. We call this
'musing' where the Muse enters or is awake

Listening to our distance from others — death is

The storm — part of the three people, alongside
or inside them. Is the car and the road

In moist woodlands

We call this musing

Members of the lungless salamander group

Breathe through their skin

Where the muse enters or is awake

Stillness keeps them alive

....

PROJECTED:

(during the car ride: onto a scrim tall as a building:
 still & moving images)

large inverted bowl

(pressure of living in air, the unbuilt
the never-to-exist)

fast windows: telephone poles, culverts, gravel

Morandi's dust-colored city of jars
sound inside the throat, dry leaves

....

on our way to the still place windows glitter like a factory

dark gray wave

grassy leaf light water to our ankles

fields curve past rutted

transparent — fiction — to believe ourselves

inside: a table & chair

turns us inside out

to a skin so legible we belong —

ditch alive with going under

scratchy with the loud grace of cicadas

Rilke's 'things' restored

here we are

widening the glass a bee on the pane

still place the storm — chalky just arr

cornfields plow into predestination

pollen count: 1,057

Iowa fertile as Egypt

sudden rain blinds the road

white milkweed or streaming hair

underwater, inside water

the number 48: invisible, named

coincidence — not made — found

Mallarmé's *figure que nul n'est*

figure that nothing is

figure that nothing births

sunflowers keel over in the heat — split faced

it's living that falls us

going down, we fight over no money

weak, ugly & unstable

stop the car to pull open the trunk

yell at each other by the side of the road

caught by the hours

ticking gears

no fear, really — just fever & the voice

out of practice but present

one hen out of sixty missed in the slaughter

returns to the site — cries out

flings herself white into the tree

what would you do

not forced (to stay alive)

not doing 'the right thing'

to freely choose

(if we can say the moon chooses)

she never runs — just turns — away

two horses in the dark

veer from the fence

exact in their empty field

trucks speed past

rolling & rolling in free will

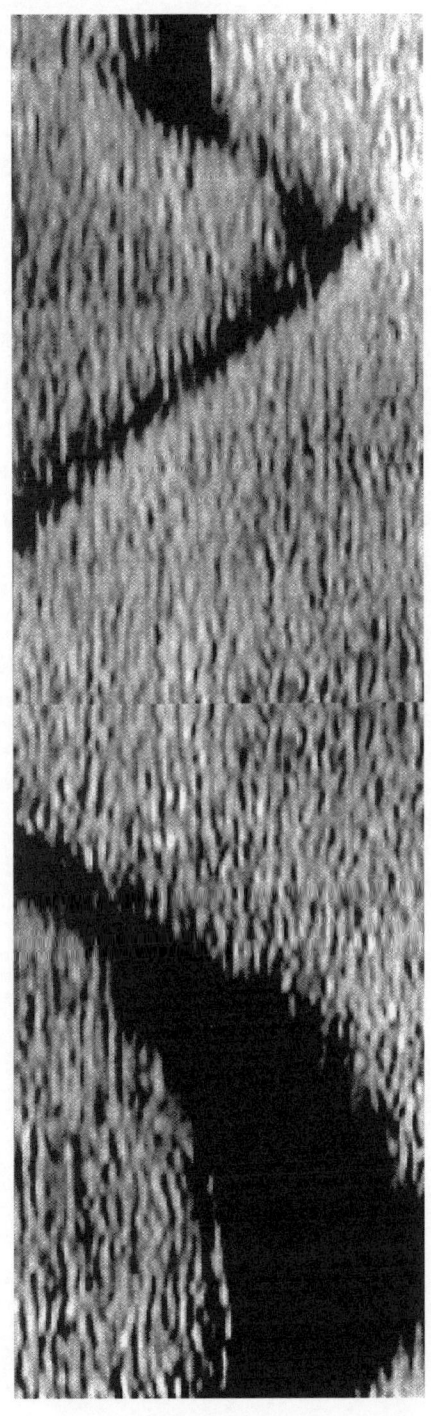

HOUSE OF SKIN:

glass block windows shaped like a human

temple of arteries, shock net of nerves

o lonesome lobby, tapestry rug

it's so stupid how things pile up:

old linotype presses, clothes that don't fit,

our successful futures — suburban, artistic

ticket stubs. rainy weather. stars. so distant.

digestion. new paint. the day his father died.

look it's no big deal. the last time we saw each other

he chased me into the street with a gun.

go back/home/where you belong

the walls constructed in trance

'you'll have all the time in the world'

AIDS saved my life — he says

turned me around from self-destruct

to live close to 'beauty' and 'art'

sound of crickets, twigs snapping

our Lady of Perpetual Heat bears down

grass pile rots in the alley

peripheral vision loosens

what's allowed to enter the lens

healing strokes: many magnetic passes

across & around the body

increments of holy air

a boy stands at the door

the head tips back

slightly — invisible spring

as the television screen goes blue

his hands on fire

bells at midnight

grainy: fast & slow

the shutter spills open

illusion of unbroken time together

in lawnchairs — in photographs

we, the future dead

embrace — touching his hand like father's wrist

what can we reach across?

to enter the living cells

fluorescing microscope limns

three-dimensional moving images

& the fourth dimension — loneliness

let me in

on the screen an egg rotates like a star

you can look inside in any direction

cells pull apart

skin separates the visible from the invisible world
the visible from the invisible word

skin· *skear, share* — to cut into —

'*fork of the body*' — like a *plowshare &*

scissors, shears: skin: *low reef, scar*

shard, car: flesh (caro)

carries us — bones & wheels

the broken line

of each self / *sheers* /

STILL : LIT

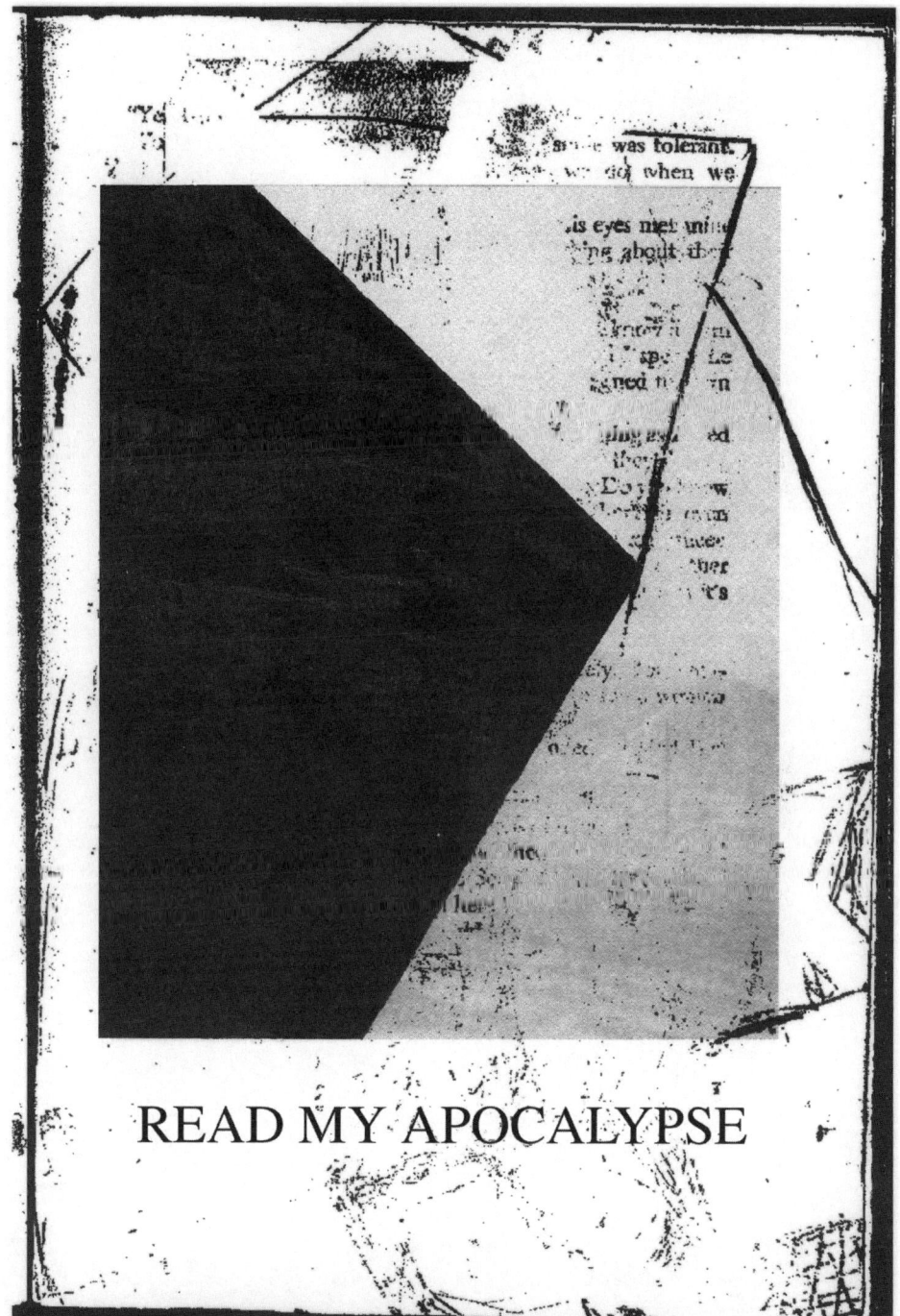

READ MY APOCALYPSE

READ MY APOCALYPSE
**a poem sequence for performance
in seven landscapes**

Niagara Falls, August 1990
Desert Shield Begins

Ganondagan, Genessee Valley
Late Summer, 1990

A Cobblestone House, Lake Geneva N.Y.

A Backyard, 1990

Amish Farmyard, Fall 1990

Broadcast Television, Winter 1990

A War Made of Videotape, January 1991

READ MY APOCALYPSE

"It was good for the nation's soul."

George Bush, November, 1991

If there were only a way back in — passageways for intervention — hinge points of choice — we could re-enter our everyday life, our own landscapes

to discover places in our lives where a distant war is decided or resisted:

national shrines, backyards, the television screen, an Amish farmyard, corporate meeting rooms — and our own hearts, the reporting we witness there and the silence.

We are not outside of history. It is necessary to locate the moments history is made: every moment. Those days from August 1990 to January 1991. Before then. And long after.

The history of the Gulf War is not over. We are writing and living it now. Where are we located? Always close to war and peace. Which will we choose?

STAGING NOTES

Throughout the performance, headlines are flashed onto the stage with slides or dot-matrix LED monitors. These appear in the text as white text, set in black boxes.

THE CHARACTERS (in order of appearance)

CHORUS: Nine or more voices (primarily women's) speaking together but not simultaneously. Cross-current of echo and resistance: a shadow chorus to the network reporters we listen to. Standing witness for the unreported, the Chorus acts as our national mirror. Members often carry mirrors on stage or in the audience and speak from the shadows — with flashlights for illumination.

HISTORIAN/TOURIST: a woman who specializes in the U.S. Labor Movement is traveling through the Northeast on vacation, during the time of Desert Shield. When she first appears, she is standing in a field of tall grasses and low shrubs — dressed in blue jeans and a t-shirt, holding a thick, tattered notebook in which she writes continuously and without hope.

WILLIAM CARLOS WILLIAMS: as a kind of tour guide or ghost who appears projected in a series of slides wearing a loose canvas jacket, chinos and glasses.

A NEW MOTHER: speaks mostly in interior monologue. She's dressed for warm weather and looks like someone you would know.

NIKÉ: winged figure: image of female power — victory for the troops — or athletic marketing emblem, depending on your point of view. She is also a projection — sometimes clearly visible, at other times fading. She ranges in size from 2 to 20 feet, resting or moving on the ground or rising to the sky of the stage.

KUAN YIN/AVALOKITESHVARA: female/male incarnation of Compassion. A non-speaking figure appearing as flames or the flickering light of millions of television sets.

FIRST LANDSCAPE: NIAGARA FALLS, AUGUST 1990
DESERT SHIELD BEGINS

Video close-up of white water falling in a repetitive loop is intercut with a car window view of the road to the falls, franchise strip along Pine Avenue in the city of Niagara Falls, near Love Canal. The sound of water runs like a wind tunnel. Continuous with traffic noise.

LOVE CANAL RENAMED AS HOMES GO ON SALE.

BUSH, HINTING FORCE, DECLARES IRAQI ASSAULT WILL NOT STAND.

LOVE CANAL CHORUS: Members of the Chorus walk toward us, each speaking in turn from Milton's Paradise Lost. *They move through shifting tableaux of images projected very large all around them from past and present conditions of the Love Canal site (as trench, greenbelt, toxic dump, elementary school and housing to resettlement) along with pictures of chromosomal data, engravings from* The Inferno, *family photos of Love Canal residents.*

These speakers are interspersed with other members of the Chorus who read matter-of-factly from the history of Love Canal, with parts of these texts also projected as running headlines to the images. Selections from these inserts can vary from performance to performance.

"As when Bands
Of Pioneers with Spade and Pickaxe armed
Forerun the Royal Camp, to trench a Field,
Or cast a Rampart.
Mammon led them on."

Originally a canal that was dug and abandoned in 1910, Love Canal became a repository for 40,000 tons of toxic waste dumped primarily by Hooker Chemical Company, along with the U.S. Army and the City of Niagara Falls between 1942 and 1953. The Canal was filled with "as much dioxin as fell on Viet Nam in the form of Agent Orange."

"Nigh on the Plain in many cells prepar'd.
That underneath had veins of liquid fire
Sluiced from the Lake."

In 1953, Love Canal was deeded to the City of Niagara Falls for $1 to become the site of the 99th St. Elementary School & the playgrounds and housing that grew around the site.

"There stood a Hill not far whose grisly top
Belch'd fire and rolling smoke . . .
Shone with a glossy scurf . . .
That in his womb was hid metallic Ore,
The work of Sulphur."

Over the years, the 40,000 tons of more than 82 chemical compounds that were buried in metal barrels in Love Canal began to corrode and leak. Surrounding neighborhoods began to reek with foul odors. Black sludge oozed from the ground and seeped from basement walls.

"Seest thou yon dreary Plain . . .
The seat of desolation, void of light"

Home owners tripped into "sinkholes of foul chemical sludge as they mowed their lawns...When a stone hit the sludge just right, a kind of smoke would rise off the surface of the muck. Sometimes the sludge itself would make a noise."

"Where all life dies, death lives, and nature breeds Perverse, all monstrous, all prodigious things."

Love Canal residents and their children began to experience "mysterious ailments, unexplained sores," epilepsy, miscarriages and stillbirths at a higher than average rate. After many studies and much litigation, Love Canal residents were moved from their homes.

A quarter of a billion dollar clean-up has left Love Canal a 40 acre "mound of clay, ringed by warning signs, a high chain link fence & drainage ditch" — an enclosed area officially known as "the reservation."

"Into this wild Abyss,
The Womb of Nature and perhaps her grave . . ."

Families began to move back to Love Canal the same weeks as Desert Shield was being unleashed in the Persian Gulf, to protect, in part the interests of Hooker Chemical — now renamed Occidental Petroleum. Love Canal was also repackaged as *Black Creek Village*. They could have called it *Paradise Lost Acres*.

WORLD-WITHOUT-END CHORUS:

our money has killed death
           (just as we outspent Communism and even Jesus)

  there's no end to anything we can buy
           — no limit at all to selling — LOVE

      CANAL REOPENS THIS WEEK, *safe as*
           anywhere, ready for the honeymoon

   safe for the mortgaged families
          washed clean by the marketplace

   washed clean and born again

RAPTURE CHORUS:

THE END OF THE WORLD
                      will easily recognize us

some ordinary day, like today

           as steam from a coffee cup rises faintly

and laundry dries, faithful & unsaved.

         As the shadow of an unbaptized child

    grows visible against the white

      vinyl siding of her mobile home

(Hiroshima was just a rehearsal)

     her dress transfixed against

    this retinal instant, emptied

echo of the radio as a woman's voice

   fades into the last mortal

      vowels we will ever hear.

Is the half-life of radium
finally set to rest?
Are the waves of the ocean
quiet now and all microbes
all protozoa, all flowery diatoms
and oxygen atoms at last
still as dead meat?

All I know is   we'll finally escape
     these crowded and bad streets
         — the freeways now calm as church.
We'll loosen our real selves
   (the ones hemmed in by years
         of low pay, insults and broken hearts)

It's all written down
                    how we'll get SNATCHED UP
        "to meet the Lord in the air"

just like the Eagle who rapts away his own, his very favorite
        trembling lamb lost in this scorched

                unsheltered field.

AND ALL THOSE LEFT BEHIND?

                the unelected, unlucky and the lost?
        where do all the animals go —
                        the birds in the air & anemones
        hidden in their shining tidepools?

            They'll be the last witnesses on earth
    sounding just like the grandmother
        who endured our bombings of Basra
        after watching her grandson die:

        "I looked in the sky and saw nothing.
                No flashes of bombs or bullets, no rubble.
        Sitting on what used to be our sitting room,

                Praise be to Allah, I have gone blind."

CHORUS   *(addressing the waters of Niagara):*

miles of sad, rotten
                              streets on the way to pure
water, O LIFE-EVERLASTING   *thou dove-winged*
      thou clear springs replenishing
                  source of white galaxied air

      of water burning itself

            alive, wild — incoherent

         oxygen collides
                  all waters awake

            to flame and echo
                              God's voice
            their Fall passionate

         complete and repetitive

            as our own

         as we drive past sour, corroded factories

            past the *Swan Motel,* past empty power plants

      a river of Jacuzzi bridal suites
                  and outdated, clumsy fuel.

         Swim deep into this — mutilated

            sanctuary of water, hidden recesses

      of mercury nitrates, potassium chloride & dioxin

               o water, forgive us —

      what is lost, falls over us, water
            green as linden leaves
      let us drown, let the earth be wet again

            with water breathing

The sound of water fades as the stage becomes clear and quiet except for one remaining member of the Chorus who speaks with her back facing us.

MEMBER OF THE CHORUS *(at times almost shouting):*

Did you see those

American workers at the hot dog stand

outside of Seneca Falls?

Flies halo their faces

the young mother smokes and perfects her desperate

boredom — in the once verdant

home of the abolitionist and women's rights movements.

Now they're coming up jobless

with plenty of things to buy

"the pure products of America"

WILLIAMS, ARE YOU LISTENING?

we've inherited your U/S/A,

driving around all day

"as if the earth under our feet were

an excrement of some sky"

INVADING IRAQIS SEIZE KUWAIT AND ITS OIL;
U.S. CONDEMNS ATTACK; URGES UNITED ACTION

SECOND LANDSCAPE: LATE SUMMER, 1990
GANONDAGAN, GENESSEE VALLEY N.Y.

Ganondagan was the site of the Village of Peace, the Seneca community & granary destroyed by the French in 1687.

The Three Sisters: corn, squash & beans were culitvated and held sacred there.

Jikohnsaseh — known as the Peace Mother for her efforts in negotiating the Iroquois Confederacy — is buried nearby.

Strong evidence points to the influence of the Iroquois Confederacy Great Law of Peace *upon the development of the U.S. Constitution.*

"IT IS ONLY THROUGH THE THREAT OF FORCE THAT A STABLE WORLD CAN BE MAINTAINED."
Senator John Danforth, Gulf War Debate

The Historian stands in a field reading from her notebook against the sound of burning which echoes in intensity the roar of Niagara. She begins by quoting lines spoken earlier by the Chorus.

THE HISTORIAN:

A slide of William Carlos Williams lying down on the grass is projected
across the field from the Historian. As she speaks, his image reappears
at intervals in different locations: writing at a desk; standing and motioning
to the audience.

Let us drown, let the earth be wet again
with water breathing

into hills and furrows, where corn
writes the history of this country

purple and white, white flint seeds

brought up the spine of the Mississippi

spilling cornmeal over water

made sacred

an awakening

we've lost all record of

"the seed as a child might be
 as a child might suffer or rejoice"

It was here the French burned the storehouses,
the wide rooms and lodge piles now grass and earth

thousands of bushels of corn — aflame

firestorm at the heart of this world
tunnel of light

radiant with death

all treasure
lives in the seed

immaculate, unseen — burning

we keep burning

what we want to own
                         the earlier napalm

igniting granaries and villages that become
                                      maps made of ashes

tracing roads into the invisible world
                    alongside us called history

                                      tangled but not altogether lost
in these pathways
                    where some animal dives, disappearing into grass, speeding
            to the underworld, the Inferno of General Denonville

right in this field where I pray through the soles of my feet

                         for healing and when the healing comes
it's as small as a pinpoint
                    spiral parasite entering the New World of my blood

as the wheel starts over

                    <goldfinch sparks off sumac and birch>

I think this place is Viet Nam — the burning fields

coincident with the long houses of the Seven Nations —

birthplace of our indigenous
                              democracy, aflame

in the midst of wild cherry and bass wood straight to the sky
            a paradise of filtered light and maples

                    <great blue heron overhead>

"it is only in isolate flecks that
something
is given off"

in the tiny seeds & spores

            history's ashes present
                    in our breath,   our blood

THIRD LANDSCAPE: A COBBLESTONE HOUSE, LAKE GENEVA, N.Y.
NEAR GANONDAGAN

A member of the Chorus sits in a plain wood chair on stage in front of the facade
of a cobblestone house projected close to life-size. The house was built by masons
who constructed the Erie Canal & is now on the edge of town being swallowed by
neighboring car lots & motels, just as the speaker is swallowed by the folds &
crevices of the stone walls projected across her.

MEMBER OF THE CHORUS:

in the tiny seeds & spores
history stays alive
undoing these cobblestone walls and wide sills, that resist our progress
"do you know this country?" the old woman asks, barely surviving
her genteel poverty and decency of upkeep:
artifacts scattered around her as at a museum display,
archeological dig: an old tub scrubber — decoratively shaped,
rubber bands saved, radiator repainted — obdurate,
ancient, unrepentant — testifying for her:
democratic meant: not worshipping the rich
USED TO BE

A FREE COUNTRY
now the TV downstairs glitters into the night, mixes with
the sound of a bee trapped by heat and a gauze curtain
as commerce wheels across America
in the grind and howling of trucks, past the future
sites of lit-up outlets
for the Three Sisters: Hamburger, Gasoline & Coke

The slide fades to a close-up of a window: old, thin, white curtain and the sound of a bee fading into fast moving traffic sounds. This scene is then replaced by the image of a city franchise strip roadway overlapping images of the Persian Gulf war zone: the road to Baghdad.

"I'M TALKING ABOUT JOBS...OIL RUNS THE ECONOMY OF THE WORLD. IT FUELS OUR FACTORIES, HEATS OUR HOMES, CARRIES OUR PRODUCTS FROM MANUFACTURE TO MARKET. IT'S AS BASIC TO THE ECONOMY AS WATER IS TO LIFE."
Senator William Roth, Gulf War Debate

FOURTH LANDSCAPE: A BACKYARD, 1990

A new mother sits in a lawnchair in a backyard near the Delaware River.
Dressed for warm weather, she is half reading a book. We overhear her
in a series of interior monologues broadcast around the theater — with
an effect much like voice-over in cinema. Her speaking shifts tone with
the freedom of complete privacy.

THE NEW MOTHER: (interior voice-over)

It's like going for days shooting a roll of film
that isn't spooled, accumulating
blank frames so living the days
without record has to be enough

Memory has no *things* in it
like dreams, it is made entirely of language

and what is language made of?

Lying in the grass,
I'm losing some of my tiredness

I can feel time
moving in all directions

> *BUSH SENDS U.S. FORCE TO SAUDI ARABIA*
> *50,000 TROOPS ARE DEPLOYED*   August, 1990

History crowds in everywhere
pushes on the graceful, long needled white pines
tangles wild grapes, ferns, blueberries and
dead-ends into the gray rock cave in these woods

There are so many roads built to arrive *here*
a place where we can remember ourselves
exactly at this moment

Skin open to the sun
yellow feather on the ground

I can feel the baby's eyes open,
needing contact every moment
very sensitive to touch — beautiful —
not sleeping much, looking for the breast everywhere

> *"HE IS WILLING TO BEND ANY LAW AND MAKE ALMOST ANY*
> *SACRIFICE TOWARDS THESE ENDS. HE IS UNPREDICTABLE*
> *AS A DESERT STORM AND AS DECEPTIVE AS A MIRAGE."*
> Senator Wm. Roth, Gulf War Debate

way out on a meadow
the deer come out sometimes
mostly they stay close to

the woods, dark moon

what I know is

my child is learning how to walk
and we're trying to stay alive

like people everywhere

new life at the center of our lives
and this large green world at peace

A television set on the ground across from the New Mother
is suddenly turned on with the image of a large cone of flame
burning in a suburban backyard.

FIFTH LANDSCAPE: AN AMISH FARMYARD, FALL 1990

The Historian stands alongside projected images of an Amish farmyard &
house. She is located to the side, as a commentator or reporter might be.

THE HISTORIAN:

in this large green world, at peace
we're all speeding backwards
into the days before war

something is growing — how terrible

each seed of this war — invisible and efficacious as laser

each seed — a door swinging open
toward rows of crimson plants floating like anemones

in our gardened memory

where chickens scatter and eddy around a woman
who wears a white kerchief and blue dress in this farmyard

> *U.S. GULF TROOPS DOUBLED TO 430,000*
> *November 8, 1990*

we're moving toward a thin green line

voice in the meadow

a listening in the leaves
called history, which unlike the news
goes back in time and allows us to change the past

The Historian's commentary continues as projected images move inside the
farmhouse to show scenes of a family preparing supper, eating together:
close-ups (a pitcher, the back of a woman turning toward the window).

in this ordinary world of plates,
bread, of faded blue clothing & water

a family sits down to eat together
wondering if we will go to war

WHERE IS OUR HUMAN
WILDERNESS REFUGE —

where is our shelter
from weapons and their deployment?

To read and write
means to feel the weight of letters

as we construct a refuge together

something growing in the fields:

winged Niké hovers over the wide desert

she's our wilderness
our refuge

she's the language living deep inside our tongue

did we give her a chance to speak?

SIXTH LANDSCAPE: BROADCAST TELEVISION, WINTER 1991

The Chorus stands in a semi-circle around a large screen t.v. which shows a tape
of what they are now speaking live. Images of Niké — miniature and very large
— are projected at various sites and angles, both on-stage and floating above.

THE CHORUS:

Did we give her a chance to speak
before the end of all flowers?

She's moving away from us

blossoming in soldiers like a lotus,
like blood red poppies, like wheat.

We send soldiers to lie in the desert
to silence our fear

we send youths to be our Shield,
we send infantry   <from the Latin for infant

meaning 'unable to speak'>

In this season of last red roses
the world stays alive in oilfields
lit incarnation
of flower — isolate heart — all objects of the senses

fallen, reeling

We're helpless except in our refusal
to live the lives of people on television
selling us our lives
— the lives we already own.

Their faces grow animated nightly
in our living rooms, flickering with light

our *semblables,* our *frères*   our selves
monitor us
with the unceasing vigilance of all the gods we've lost

our shrines aflame with burning oil, without end, without hope front page, N.Y. Times, January 11, 1991

CONGRESS NEARS WAR DEBATE AS BUSH SIDE GAINS

RICH GOT RICHER IN 80'S

"OUR ONLY HOPE IS BY GIVING THE PRESIDENT THE RIGHT TO USE FORCE, HE WILL NOT HAVE TO USE THAT FORCE"

January 12

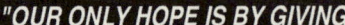

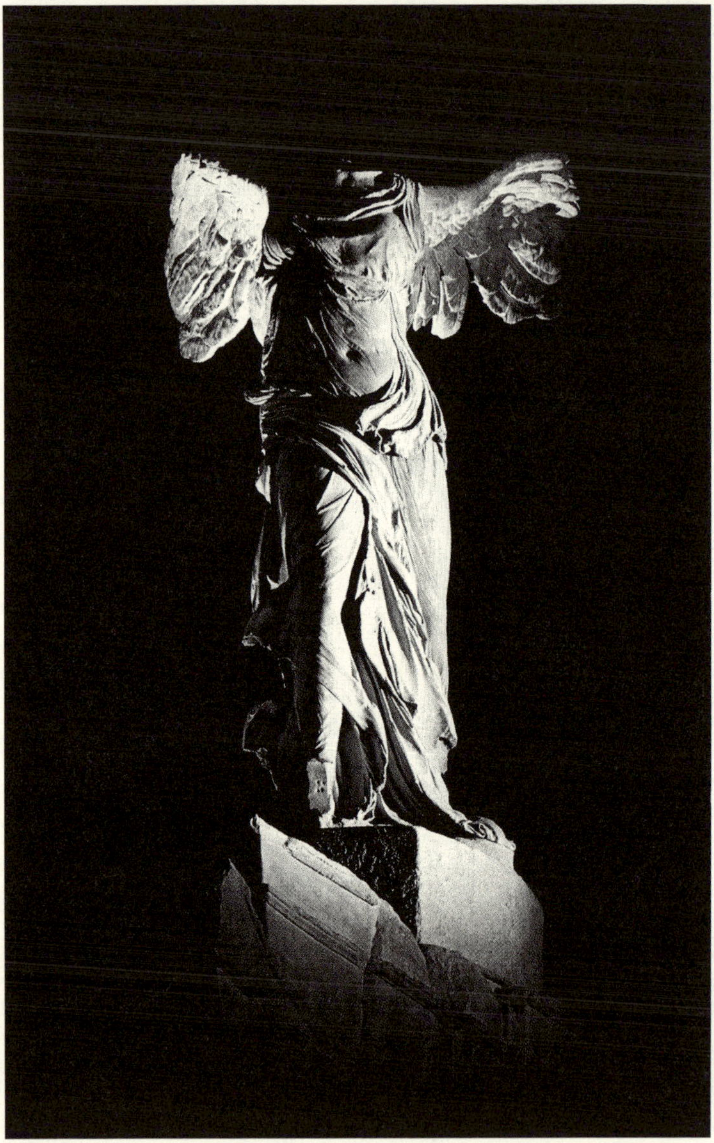

The stage darkens and echoes with the soundtrack lead-in for network news coverage of the Gulf/Showdown/Stand-off/Crisis. Lights focus on the reassembled Chorus who stand in a room with no walls, formed at four corners by upright poles. Two large video screens are centered side by side in front of the Chorus. The winged Niké figure is projected above the open room. Her image grows in size and intensity as the Chorus speaks.

SEVENTH LANDSCAPE: A WAR MADE OF VIDEOTAPE, JANUARY 1991

While the Chorus speaks, the unwalled room onstage has begun to catch on fire: the posts at each corner, and then a thin perimeter of flame marking a rectangle between the posts, burns like the emerging thin line of a prairie fire. The Chorus speaks inside the burning structure, at differing pace, tone and with uncanny clarity.

CHORUS *(in a full range of vocal registers & timing):*

Without hope, without end,

our Lady of Victory fades into a figure that is either

disappearing or emerging,

it's hard to tell in this video dust.

She says   *to take care of life*   is all we can do

a vow or vowel

to love our enemy selves.

One video screen is filled with the image of a stone; the other with that of a plain white cup. As the Chorus continues, each object bursts into flame.

That cry — we are

facing in the warm large wind

as two moons rise in one month —

a terrible fertility of missiles

human-made comets, flawed and lethal

waiting for our sky to open

no division between

paper and the fire that can burn

each person on earth

alive

trembling   heart,

awake

As the Chorus closes, one video screen carries the repeated bombing of an Iraqi target shown from the air; the other screen is filled with waters pouring over Niagara.

The soundtrack carries the roar of water & fire on opposite sides of the theater. Headlines are projected over the length of the stage in succession.

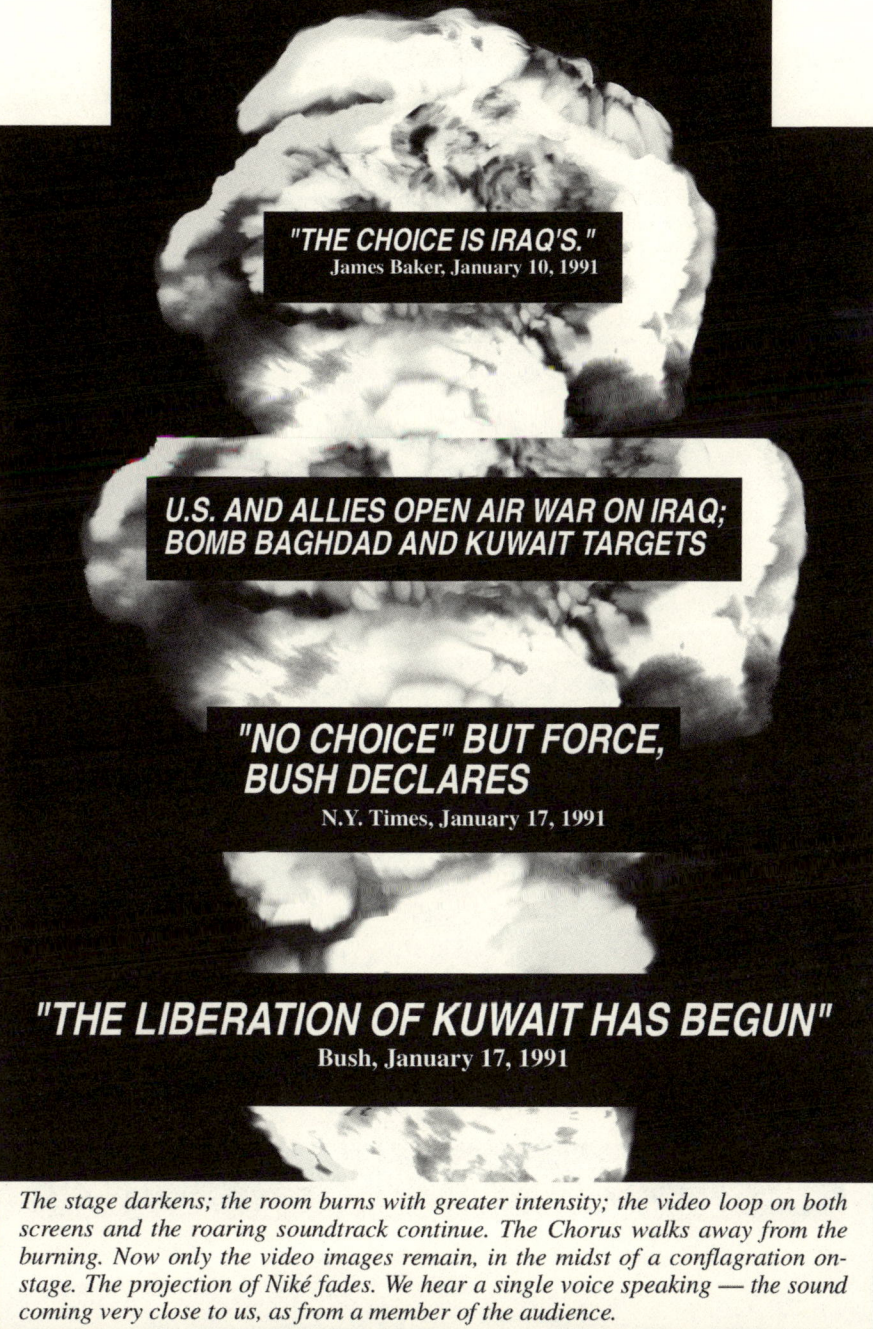

"THE CHOICE IS IRAQ'S."
James Baker, January 10, 1991

**U.S. AND ALLIES OPEN AIR WAR ON IRAQ;
BOMB BAGHDAD AND KUWAIT TARGETS**

**"NO CHOICE" BUT FORCE,
BUSH DECLARES**
N.Y. Times, January 17, 1991

"THE LIBERATION OF KUWAIT HAS BEGUN"
Bush, January 17, 1991

The stage darkens; the room burns with greater intensity; the video loop on both screens and the roaring soundtrack continue. The Chorus walks away from the burning. Now only the video images remain, in the midst of a conflagration on-stage. The projection of Niké fades. We hear a single voice speaking — the sound coming very close to us, as from a member of the audience.

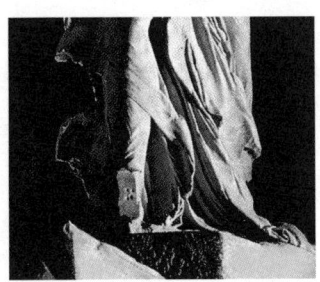

MEMBER OF THE CHORUS *(SPEAKING AS FROM THE AUDIENCE):*

And who - will begin - our liberation from Force?

END

Notes

Front Matter

(vii) *"Theater of the Mind"* by Shelley Berc appeared in *Exquisite Corpse*, vol. 7 and is excerpted here with the author's permission.

The Poor Body

Performance, PostMasters Gallery, New York, New York, 1986 choreographed and performed by Elizabeth Lahey; text, sound and stills by Meredith Stricker; videography by Frederic Lahey.

The Lightning Hive

Quotations

(17) *"this excessive hieraticism with its sliding alphabet . . ."* Antonin Artaud: "For The Theater And Its Double" in *Antonin Artaud Selected Writings*, edited by Susan Sontag; University of California Press; 1988: p. 226

(19) *"Orpheus irrelevant to her rising"* Jane Harrison, *Themis*.

(24) *"thy floating singer late"* Hart Crane from "Atlantis" in *The Bridge*.

(28) *"bees see a color we cannot even imagine"* H. Munroe Fox, *The Personality of Animals*.

(28) *"a light and winged and holy thing"* Plato, *Ion*.

(31) *"Tie a string to a bit of wood & whirl it over your head at initiation rites"* Jane Harrison, *Themis*.

(31) *"roars from the unseen"* Jane Harrison, *Themis*.

(32) *"Here I am"* A.P. Report, Iowa City *Press Citizen*, summer 1987.

(32) *"There was no thunder, lightning or sign of lightning before the killer bolt struck"* A.P. Report, Iowa City *Press Citizen*, summer 1987.

(33) *"The sacred is the father of god"* Jane Harrison quoting Durkheim in *Themis*.

(34) *"We are the bees of the Invisible"* Rilke, *Letters*.

(34) *"The feare of things invisible is the naturall seed of religion"* Hobbes, quoted by Jane Harrison in *Themis*.

(34) *"a shy bird hard to catch"* Jane Harrison, *Themis*.

(34) *"a fragment of anything to its entirety"* Jane Harrison, *Themis*.

Images

(15) *Drawing* by the author.

(16) *"the bee hum of all languages"* video stills and graphics by the author.

(27) *"The bee's language"* video stills and graphics by the author.

(36) *"silence is the active rain"* video stills and graphics by the author.

(37–42) *For staging notes* drawings and final bees/letters by the author.

The Still Place

Images

(43) *From electron microscope* print by Steve Stricker.

(44) *Drawing* by the author.

(47) *Photo* of Maze performance with Elizabeth Lahey and the author, 1980.

(53) *Cornfield* video still and scan by the author.

(56) *Snow on lilacs* video still and scan by the author.

(58) *Scissors, grass, light* Maze performance, with Elizabeth Lahey and the author, 1980.

Read My Apocalypse

(61–84) *The boxed quotation/headlines* throughout the text are gathered from the *New York Times*, during the period of preparation for the Gulf War known as "Desert Shield."

(61) "READ MY APOCALYPSE" anti war sign quoted by Grace Paley in "Something About The Peace Movement," from *The Gulf Between Us*, edited by Victoria Brittain.

(61) *"It was good for the nation's soul"* George Bush quoted in a speech at Arlington Cemetery, by Linda Ellerbe, *Des Moines Register*, November 14, 1992.

First Landscape: Niagara Falls/Love Canal

(64–68) References for the chorus section: Dante: *The Divine Comedy, Volume One: The Inferno;* translated by Mark Musa, Penguin, New York; 1984. Michael Kronewetter, *Managing Toxic Wastes;* Julian Messner: Englewood Cliffs, New Jersey, 1989. Milton, *Paradise Lost* and *Paradise Regained;* edited by C. Ricks; Penguin: New York; 1968. Pat Robertson: *The New World Order;* Word Publishing; Dallas, 1991. Rebecca Stefoff, *Environmental Disasters;* Chelsea House Publishers; New York. Charles B. Strouer, *Apocalypse: On the Psychology of Fundamentalism in America;* Beacon; New York; 1997. Malcom Weiss, *Toxic Waste: Clean Up or Cover Up;* Watts: New York; 1984.

(64) *quotations in boldface* are from Milton's *Paradise Lost* and *Paradise Regained*, edited by C. Ricks, Penguin, 1968.

(64) *"as much dioxin . . ."* Verlyn Klinkenborg, "Back To Love Canal," *Harper's Magazine*, March 1991, p. 71.

(64) *"mound of clay . . ."* Michael Brown, "A Toxic Ghost Town," *Atlantic Monthly*, July 1989, p. 23.

(67) *"I looked in the sky and saw nothing . . ."* Um-Rashid, resident of Basra, during the 1991 Gulf War, quoted in "Tales of War: Arab Women in the Eye of the Storm," in *The Gulf Between Us,* edited by Victoria Brittain, Virago, London, 1991, p.9.

(69) *"as if the earth under our feet . . ."* William Carlos Williams from section XVIII in *Spring and All, Imaginations*, New York, N.Y. : New Directions, 1970: pp. 131, 132.

Second Landscape: Ganondagan, Genessee Valley

(70) *Ganondagan* see "Iroquoian Political Concept and the Genesis of American Government" by Donald Grinde in Northeast Indian Quarterly, *American Indian Program*, Cornell University, Winter 1989.

(70) *Senator Danforth,* Congressional Debate on the Gulf War, excerpted in the *New York Times,* Jan. 11, 1991.

(71) *"the seed as a child might be as a child might suffer or rejoice,"* based on a quotation in an article by Roderico Terni, "Cosmological Importance of Corn Among Mayan Peoples": "In that sense, corn is looked upon as a living being, as a child might be, in the same way as us humans—a being that can suffer, that can talk with us, that can cry," translated by José Barreiro in "Indian Corn of the Americas: Gift to the World," *Northeast Indian Quarterly*; spring/summer 1989; Cornell University.

(72) *the Inferno of Denonville* General Denonville led the French attack on the Seneca fort of Gay-a-yan-duk (or Ganondagan), destroying the extensive village and granaries in 1687.

(72) *"it is only in isolate flecks that . . ."* William Carlos Williams, from Section XVIII of *Spring and All.*

Third Landscape: Lake Geneva

(74) *"the pure products..."* William Carlos Williams, from Section XVIII of *Spring and All.*

(74) *Senator Roth,* Congressional Debate on the Gulf War, excerpted in the *New York Times,* Jan. 11, 1991.

Seventh Landscape: Broadcast Television

(81) *to take care of life* based on a quotation by Dainin Katagiri: "To take care of life is to burn with the flame of life," in *Returning to Silence: Zen Practice in Daily Life,* Shambala, Boston, 1988: p. 27.

Images

(59) Digital collage by the author base on stealth bomber wing.

(61) Photograph digitally reworked by the author to represent burning oil fields during the Gulf War.

(63) First landscape: Niagara Falls, antique postcard, Love Canal.

(70) Second landscape: corn, original photo, Thom Cowen.

(74) Third landscape: Drawing of the Road To Baghdad, Gulf War, by the author.

(80) Sixth landscape: Niké, based on a postcard, author's collection.

(82) Seventh landscape: Oil well on fire, digital image by the author; Niagara Falls, antique postcard, author's collection.

(84) Niké, based on a postcard in the author's collection.

About the author: Meredith Stricker is an artist and poet living on California's Central Coast. Working as a partner in an art and architecture studio, she is developing the Center for Visual Poetry to bring together artists, writers, and experimental forms. She has been selected for the 2002 National Poetry Series Award.